ROLLS-ROYCE

LEADER IN LUXURY

by
JERRY CRAVEN
and
LINDA CRAVEN

THE ROURKE CORPORATION, INC.
Vero Beach, FL 32964

Cover photograph: The original 1907 Silver Ghost, the most famous Rolls-Royce.

ACKNOWLEDGMENTS

We are grateful to Rolls-Royce, Ltd. for supplying the photographs for this book. We are especially grateful to Mr. David Preston and Mr. Jack Bunting for their invaluable assistance in helping us understand Rolls-Royce automobiles.

Library of Congress Cataloging-in-Publication Data

Craven, Jerry.
    Rolls-Royce: leader in luxury / by Jerry Craven and Linda Craven.
        p. cm. – (Car classics)
    Includes index.
    Summary: Gives a brief history of the Rolls-Royce automobile and describes its special features and classic models.
    ISBN 0-86593-147-X
    1. Rolls-Royce automobile – Juvenile literature. [1. Rolls-Royce automobile.] I. Craven, Linda. II. Title. III. Series: Car classics (Vero Beach, Fla.)
TL215.R6C73 1991
629.222'2–dc20
                                         91-10000
                                           CIP
                                           AC

CONTENTS

CHAPTER 1

THE BEST CAR IN THE WORLD

Right: Ladies and gentlemen arrive at the opera in an early Rolls-Royce.

Left: Today's Rolls-Royces combine classic design with high-tech performance.

The Queen of England has a Rolls-Royce. So do other members of her royal family, and so do many rich and famous people the world over.

Since 1904, many people have called Rolls-Royce the best car in the world. Rolls-Royces have been driven by sultans, sheikhs, kings, queens, movie stars, and captains of industry. The Phantom VI Rolls was sold exclusively to royalty and heads of state; only 16 were ever built.

During the company's first 35 years, the goal of Rolls-Royce designers was to build the best machine possible. Cost was not a factor.

Until 1939, anyone who wanted a Rolls-Royce purchased the chassis (the working part) from the Rolls factory and then ordered a custom-built body from a coach builder.

In 1921, Otto Oppenheimer, a dealer in diamonds, ordered a Rolls-Royce with a secret compartment for carrying diamonds. He gave his car a name – The Black Diamond.

The Sheikh of Kuwait owned two Rolls in 1956, one for each end of the twenty-mile stretch of road in his country.

Today, many people still consider the Rolls-Royce the best car in the world. Certainly it is one of the most expensive. A new model costs around $200,000.

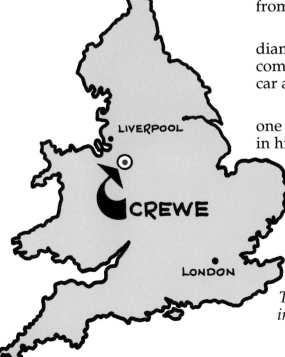

The Rolls-Royce factory is located at Crewe, in the heart of England.

CHAPTER 2

THE FOUNDERS

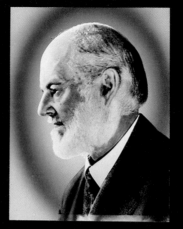

Founders Charles Rolls (left) and Henry Royce were of different ages and backgrounds, but they made a good team.

The automotive genius behind the early Rolls-Royce cars was Henry Royce. He grew up poor in England and at age 10 had a job selling newspapers. Royce loved tinkering with machines, especially electric motors. In 1902, he owned a successful electrical business, and he bought a used car.

The car he chose was a French 1901 Décauville, a noisy, rattly, and unreliable vehicle. A self-taught engineer, Royce decided he could build a better automobile in his shop. He built three 10 horsepower (hp) cars during 1903 and 1904.

Charles Rolls on the 20 hp model that won the Tourist Trophy in 1906

Charles Stuart Rolls, a young aristocrat, was so impressed with Royce's cars that he offered to sell them. The two men formed a partnership called Rolls-Royce Motor Cars.

Rolls, who had the connections to sell cars, described Royce as "the greatest motor-car engineer in the world." Rolls enjoyed field-testing the company cars, and he won a number of cross-country races in the early models.

Businessman Claude Johnson has often been called "the hyphen" in the Rolls-Royce company name. Also a partner in Rolls-Royce, he managed the company and helped make it into a financial success.

Charles Rolls died in a plane crash in 1910. Henry Royce, until his death in 1933, controlled the development and mechanical design of all models the company built.

The Rolls-Royce stand at a 1906 motor show

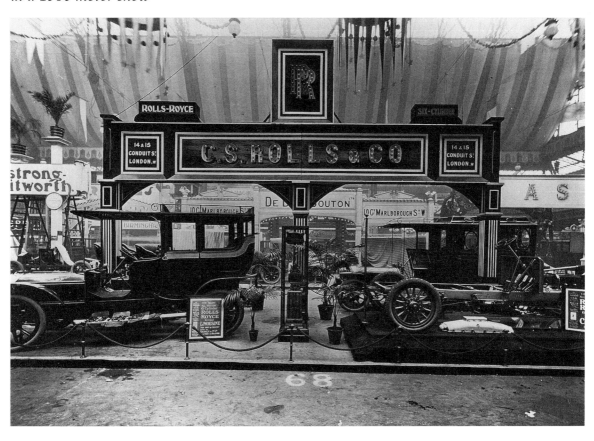

CHAPTER 3

THE EARLY ROLLS-ROYCES

From 1904 to 1906, the new Rolls-Royce company built a 10 horsepower car. Barker and Company, a popular English coach builder, built the bodies to customer order.

The 10 horsepower was the only two-cylinder auto produced in England at the time, and it was the quietest and most reliable of any two cylinder car in the world. For the era, it would go astonishingly fast: 38 miles per hour.

Royce experimented with other models in the early years. He built an Invisible Engine model with a V-8 engine hidden under the floorboard. Only three were built; the V-8 engine was not reintroduced until 1959.

Another early experiment was the Legalimit model, a car that would not go over 20 miles per hour, the legal speed limit in England at the time. It, too, was soon discontinued.

More successful was the 20 horsepower car called the Light 20. In 1906, Charles Rolls, driving from Monte Carlo to London, beat a previous world record by one and one-half minutes even though he waited three hours for a boat to take him across the English Channel.

Royce personally directed all Rolls-Royce development until his death in 1933.

Charles Rolls liked the heat of competition.

Henry Royce built the world's best two-cylinder car.

10 hp model, 1904-1906

Engine type	Cast-iron fixed head monoblock, on aluminum crankcase
No. of cylinders	2
Bore/stroke mm	95.2 X 127
Sparkplugs per cyl.	1
Compression ratio	3:1
Clutch	Cone
Transmission	Separate 3-speed gearbox
Brakes	Rear only; footbrake operating on transmission; handbrake internal expanding on rear wheels
Wheels	Artillery with wooden spokes
Max. speed	38 mph
Number built	16

CHAPTER 4

THE SILVER GHOST

Royce's 40/50 chassis design was so good that it stayed in production until 1925.

In 1906, Henry Royce designed what he later considered to be the best car he ever built – the 40/50 horsepower model. The car was so successful that Rolls-Royce discontinued all other models from 1907 to 1922, making only what came to be known as the Silver Ghost.

Claude Johnson promoted the 40/50 model by having the thirteenth one they built painted silver. He also used genuine silver plate for the trim and called the car the Silver Ghost – silver for its color and ghost for how quietly the car ran.

That original Silver Ghost was sold and driven over 500,000 miles before the Rolls-Royce company bought it back in 1948. Since then it has been on display at Rolls-Royce and is now in the company showroom in Crewe, England. It is still sometimes taken out on tour.

In an era of noisy cars, the 40/50 astonished everyone with its silence. American customs inspectors at first refused to believe that the initial

The Silver Ghost models were favorites of the leisure class.

Silver Ghost imports had an internal-combustion engine. Surely, they argued, anything so quiet must be electric.

Rolls-Royce built the last of the Silver Ghosts in 1925. During 19 years of producing the model, Henry Royce continually improved the car, and coach builders made a host of elegant and luxurious body designs.

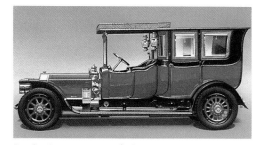

J. A. Lawton and Co. built this 1911 Silver Ghost body.

The Silver Ghost: the 40/50 hp model 1906-1925

Engine type	2 cast-iron fixed head monoblocks
No. of cylinders	2
Bore/stroke mm	114.3 X 114.3
Displacement cc	7036 (7428 in later models)
Sparkplugs per cyl.	2
Clutch	Cone
Transmission	Separate 4-speed gearbox; 3-speed gearbox in 1910
Brakes	Rear only until 1924
Wheels	Artillery with wooden spokes available to 1921; wire in 1913
Max. speed	69 mph
Number built	6173 in England; 1700 in the U.S.

CHAPTER 5

FROM CARS TO TANKS AND PLANES

*Rolls-Royce armored cars
served in both World War I
and World War II.*

With the outbreak of World War I in 1914, the Rolls-Royce company ceased making cars for civilian use and turned to the manufacture of war machinery.

Silver Ghost-based armored cars entered combat in the first year of the war and by the end had seen action on every front. The 40/50 tank was essentially a regular Silver Ghost chassis outfitted with steel plating and a Vickers .303 machine gun. The car carried a crew of four.

Twin rear wheels helped cope with the additional weight of the armor. The radiator was protected from bullets with steel doors that could be closed during combat. Closing the doors protected the cooling system but caused the cars to overheat.

This Rolls-Royce Merlin engine was the best aircraft engine used by the British in World War II.

In 1915, when the crew of the British ship *Tara* was held by Senussi tribesmen on the Sahara desert, the Duke of Westminster rescued them using 45 armored cars, mostly Rolls-Royces. The cars traveled day and night to save the British seamen; the popular mission enhanced the reputation of the Rolls-Royce company. The famous English soldier, T. E. Lawrence, known as Lawrence of Arabia, praised the Silver Ghost tanks for dependability and endurance in his book *The Seven Pillars of Wisdom.*

Early in World War II some of the old Rolls-Royce armored cars were still in service. All auto production ceased, and the Rolls factory produced war materials, mainly airplane engines.

Sixteen people died when Nazis bombed the Rolls-Royce plant in 1940.

CHAPTER 6

THE BABY ROLLS

This 1922 Baby Rolls was sold to the Maharana of Udaipur in India.

During the slow economic years following World War I, Claube Johnson led the Rolls-Royce company to produce a smaller, less expensive car. The new car was called the Twenty because it had a 20 horsepower engine; it was made from 1922 to 1929. People nicknamed it "the Baby Rolls." Ever since, the company has made two models – one large, one small. Many people still refer to the smaller model as the baby.

Henry Royce developed a new engine for the Twenty, one with overhead valves similar to those on many American cars. The car was shorter and lower to the ground than the Silver Ghost, and it cost one-third less. One distinctive feature was the horizontal radiator shutters, perhaps inspired by the American Hudson Super Six.

This was Lady Hambury's 1932 20/25 model. The British government took it from her for use in World War II.

Only 491 Wraiths were built before the war halted car production.

In 1929, the 20/25 model, with a 4257 cubic centimeter (cc) engine, replaced the original Baby Rolls. It could go 77 miles per hour, beating the 20 horsepower model by 17 mph.

In 1936, Rolls-Royce made the 25/30. This model was in production for only two years when it was replaced by the Wraith.

In order to cut production costs, the Wraith had a welded, rather than riveted, chassis. It had a smaller 4167 cc, six-cylinder engine. Rolls-Royce had made 491 Wraiths when World War II started in 1939, once again stopping all car production.

The Baby Rolls was reborn after the war in the form of the Silver Wraith.

This elegant 25/30 drophead coupe was owned by a film producer.

THE FIRST PHANTOMS

In 1925, the New Phantom (later called Phantom I) replaced the Silver Ghost. The New Phantom was little more than the Silver Ghost chassis with a new engine in it. It was a 7668 cc, six-cylinder engine with push-rod overhead valves. Like the Ghost, it had two spark plugs per cylinder. Its top speed was 78 mph. During its four-year production life 2,212 were built.

In 1929, the Phantom II appeared. It was the last design that Henry Royce saw completed before his death. He lowered the car's body nine inches. Though the engine size did not change from that of the Phantom I, Royce improved the car's performance enough to increase its maximum speed to 92 mph.

During the era of the Phantom II, Rolls-Royce bought Bentley Motors. The luxurious Bentley is still available from Rolls-Royce today.

When Rolls-Royce built the Phantom III, it chose a V-12 engine, likely because of its popularity in such American luxury cars as Cadillac, Lincoln, and Packard. Rolls-Royce made few of these big cars because world-wide economic problems affected the ability of even very rich people to buy luxury cars. The Phantom III was extremely expensive. It was the last model Rolls-Royce made without regard for costs.

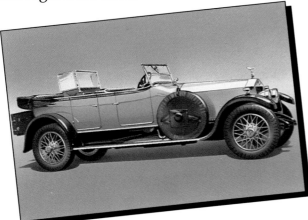

The Phantom I had a three-speed gearbox.

This 1932 four-door Phantom II spent many years in Hong Kong before being returned to England in 1976.

This one-of-a-kind body on a 1937 Phantom III has electrically operated windows.

Phantom III (1935-1939)

Engine type	Hinduminum combined crankcase and block
No. of cylinders	12
Bore/stroke mm	82.5 X 114.3
Displacement cc	7340
Sparkplugs per cyl.	2
Clutch	Single dry plate
Transmission	Separate 4-speed gearbox
Brakes	4-wheel internal expanding with mechanical servo
Wheels	Wire
Maximum speed	86.96 mph
Number built	717

CHAPTER 8

AMERICAN-BUILT ROLLS-ROYCES

Claude Johnson decided in 1919 that the United States could become an important market for Rolls-Royce. The import tax on foreign cars at the time was 33 percent, which discouraged wealthy Americans from ordering a Rolls-Royce from England. Building a factory in the U.S. would eliminate the tax.

Johnson chose Springfield, Massachusetts for the factory. The area had workers accustomed to making precision instruments. Springfield produced many of the rifles and pistols sold worldwide.

In 1921, workers in the new Springfield plant completed the first U.S.-built chassis. It was driven to a coach builder to be outfitted with a body.

But the car was an expensive one. Even with no import duty, the American-built Silver Ghost cost twice as much as a V-12 Packard and three times more than a straight-eight Cadillac.

The plant used the British design, placing the steering wheel on the right side. Although it made driving more difficult, some Americans liked the prestige of owning an English-style car with a right-hand drive. In 1925, however, the Springfield factory began building cars with the steering wheel on the left, like other American-built cars. By the time the plant closed in 1933, the majority of the cars built there – 1,890 out of 2,990 – had left-hand drives.

Right: Financial manager Claude Johnson masterminded the building of a Rolls-Royce plant in the United States.

This Springfield-made Silver Ghost used some American parts, such as the starter motor.

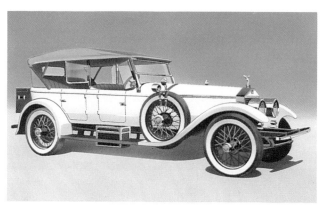

CHAPTER 9

AFTER WORLD WAR II

Because Rolls-Royce produced warplane engines, Nazis bombed the Rolls-Royce factory. When the war ended, the company had to rebuild.

Rolls-Royce made cars in a different way after the war. The biggest change was the introduction of standardized body work. Until 1939, a customer buying a Rolls-Royce bought the chassis from Rolls-Royce and the body from a separate coach builder. After World War II, the Rolls-Royce company integrated these two components.

The first Rolls-Royce made after the war was the Silver Wraith, a refinement of the pre-war Wraith. The company did not resume big-car production until 1950 with the Phantom VI, sold only to royalty and heads of state.

The Silver Dawn, produced from 1951 to 1955, marked the beginning of Rolls-Royce's policy of making one body to be used for both a Rolls-Royce and a Bentley. The only difference was that the Bentley did not get the fancy radiator that had become the hallmark of a Rolls-Royce.

In 1951, the Silver Dawn was available with an automatic transmission, patterned after the four-speed General Motors gearbox. The transmission became standard for the Silver Cloud in 1955. The Silver Cloud II, built in 1959, was the first Rolls-Royce since the Invisible Engine model of 1905 to have a V-8 engine.

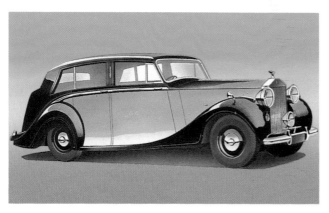

This 1948 Silver Wraith has traveled over 144,000 miles with only minor repairs.

This 1955 Silver Dawn has silk rope trim and a mohair rug in the rear compartment.

This 1958 Silver Cloud had an automatic transmission, power steering, and air conditioning.

CHAPTER 10

AMAZING FACTS

The original 1907 Silver Ghost has traveled over half a million miles and is still going.

❑ Approximately two-thirds of the 110,000 Rolls-Royce cars made since Henry Royce built his first car in 1904 are still in running condition today.

❑ The oldest known Rolls-Royce still in running order is a 1904 10 hp car owned by Thomas Love in Scotland.

❑ The first Rolls-Royce was road tested on April 1, 1904, but the company put March 31 on its press report to prevent anyone from thinking the test might be an April Fool's Day joke.

❑ A Texan, Captain Hutton, bought the first Rolls-Royce sold in America in 1906.

❑ After company manager Claude Johnson named his 1907 car "The Silver Ghost," the word "silver" has been used for six other models: Silver Dawn, Silver Wraith, Silver Cloud, Silver Shadow, Silver Spur, and Silver Spirit.

This is one of three remaining 1904 10 hp models.

❑ Co-founder Charles Rolls was the first Englishman to be killed in an airplane crash.

❑ The throttle linkage ball joints on the contemporary Rolls-Royce were originally designed by Henry Royce. No one has yet invented an improvement.

❑ The odometer of current Rolls-Royces will go up to one million miles, proof of the company's confidence in the durability of the car. The original Silver Ghost, on display at the Rolls-Royce factory in Crewe, has gone over half a million miles since it was built in 1907.

Careful testing assures high quality in every Rolls-Royce built.

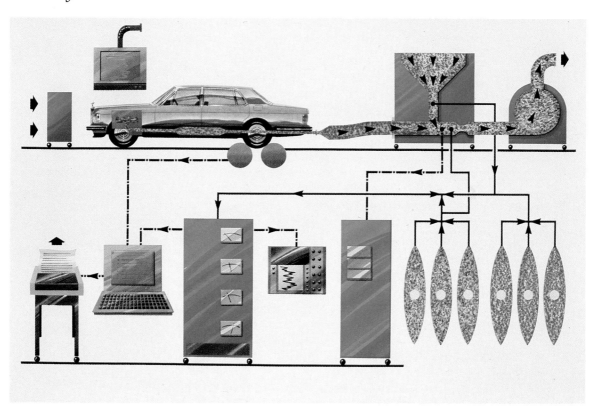

CHAPTER 11

FUN FACTS

❏ An Australian sheep farmer often transported sheep in his Rolls-Royce. He had a sliding partition installed between the front and back seats to keep the sheep from licking his ears when he drove.

❏ Another farmer sometimes took pigs to market in his elegant Rolls-Royce. "Pigs paid for it," he said. "Pigs are going to ride in it!"

❏ The Maharajah of Mysore insisted that his Rolls-Royce be blessed yearly by showering it with rose petals.

❏ Extras that customers have had fitted into their Rolls-Royces include hot and cold running water, a coffee machine, a bed, an interior roof depicting the heavens, a toilet, and a player piano.

❏ The body of a modern Rolls-Royce will sink only one and one-half inches if loaded with a full-grown African elephant. However, the company discourages such a test.

❏ The cooling power of the air conditioner in the Rolls-Royce Silver Spirit is equal to that of 30 refrigerators. You could drive a Rolls-Royce from the Arctic to the equator without adjusting the air conditioning, and the inside temperature would remain the same.

❏ Rolls-Royce tests the durability of its seats with Squirming Irma. Irma is a 200-pound simulated human bottom that tests by squirming one million times on the seat.

Above: This 1925 20 hp model sat in ruin for 29 years before it was restored and entered in a recent world rally.

Right: The exclusive Phantom VI was built and sold only to royalty and heads of state.

When women first came to work in the Rolls-Royce factory, male workers went on a week-long protest strike.

CHAPTER 12

WHAT MAKES THE ROLLS-ROYCE SO EXPENSIVE?

Rolls-Royce does not use a conveyer belt in its factory. Craftsmen move their parts to the next station only after taking the time needed to complete a perfect job.

Also, there are no robots involved in assembly, as in the making of other cars. Because each car is hand-built, it takes from three to six months to complete a single automobile.

Craftsmen assemble each engine by hand; upon completion, the engine is tested for eight hours. A specialist listens for noise with a stethoscope.

A craftsman at the Rolls-Royce plant checks the moisture content of wood.

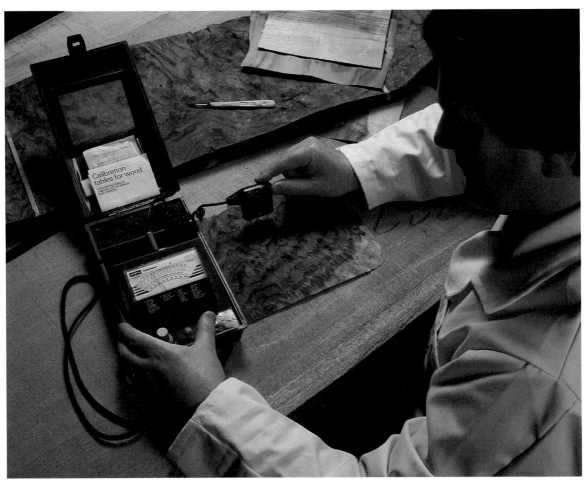

Like all wooden accessories for Rolls-Royce cars, this picnic table is sanded by hand.

The picnic table is one of the many luxury items available in a Rolls-Royce.

Many people assume the famous Rolls-Royce radiator is made of silver. Instead it's stainless steel finished to a silver sheen by five hours of hand-polishing.

For the seat covers, Rolls-Royce uses only Scandinavian hides from cattle raised within electric fences because barbed wire can scar the hides.

Specialized woodworkers build the instrument panel coverings from Italian and California walnut. They spend hours matching wood grain and finishing the wood so it is smoother than glass.

Each car gets many coats of paint, and each coat is hand sprayed, then hand rubbed. No other car manufacturer puts as many worker-hours into producing a car as Rolls-Royce.

CHAPTER 13

ROLLS-ROYCE IN THE TWENTY-FIRST CENTURY

The Rolls-Royce company has always had a policy of using the best and newest technology. At the same time, it also keeps the best traditions from its past. In the future, the company will continue to concentrate on improving the luxury and mechanics of each year's model rather than changing the body design.

The contemporary Rolls-Royce has a number of innovative devices. One button on the instrument panel checks the oil level, another opens the fuel cap. An electronic eye on the front bumper warns of icy road conditions. The ashtray empties itself automatically into a special trash bin.

Cellular phones, standard on two models, are built into the central armrest. The tool kit comes equipped with white gloves to protect hands when changing a tire.

If your family had a Rolls-Royce, the taller drivers in the family wouldn't have to readjust the seat each time they drove. A computer chip in the car remembers preferred distance and tilt. A touch of a button resets the seat. The chip also remembers and changes the outside mirror setting for each driver.

Future Rolls-Royces will use even more advanced computer chips to make the cars perform better and improve comfort for driver and passengers.

The Spirit of Ecstasy has ridden atop the hood of Rolls-Royces since 1911 and will ride there into the twenty-first century.

Right: New Rolls-Royces retain some traditional body lines.

Computer technology aids in advanced design.

CHAPTER 14

IMPORTANT DATES

1904 Rolls-Royce road tests its first car, a 10 horsepower model.

1907 Production begins on the 40/50 model, later named the Silver Ghost.

1914 Rolls-Royce stops building cars to build airplane engines and armored cars for use in World War I. Car production resumes in 1919.

1921 Rolls-Royce begins manufacturing cars in the United States.

1922 Rolls-Royce adds a new model, the Twenty, a 20 hp car called by many "the Baby Rolls."

1925 The Phantom I replaces the Silver Ghost.

1929 The Phantom II evolves from the Phantom I. The Twenty becomes the 20/25, a car with a larger engine.

1933 The United States plant closes after producing 2,990 cars in 12 years.

1936 Rolls-Royce introduces the 25/30 hp car. The Phantom III comes out with a V-12 engine.

1938 The Wraith replaces the 25/30.

1939 Rolls-Royce stops car production to build airplane engines for warplanes.

1946 The Silver Wraith is the new Baby Rolls. Rolls-Royce begins offering its cars with standard body work for the first time.

1949 With the Silver Dawn, Rolls-Royce begins building its own car bodies produced wholly at the Crewe plant in England.

1950 The Phantom VI is offered only to heads of state and royalty.

1955 The Silver Cloud is the last six-cylinder Rolls-Royce. The Silver Cloud II in 1959 and the Silver Cloud III in 1962 have V-8 engines.

1959 The Phantom V, built until 1968, brings the Phantom line of cars to an end.

1965 Rolls-Royce introduces the Silver Shadow. The Silver Shadow II comes out in 1977, the same year as the Silver Wraith II, which is simply a Silver Shadow with a longer wheelbase.

1975 The Camargue enters production, a top-line luxury sedan.

1980 The Silver Spirit offers luxury and speed. It will go from 0 to 60 mph in 10 seconds.

1985 A limited production of 25 Silver Spur Centenary models are built to celebrate the birth of automobiles a century before.

1989 The Silver Spirit II offers greater luxury with a refined suspension system.

1990 The Silver Spur II comes with a telephone built into the armrest.

This 1929 Phantom II was temporarily rebodied as an ambulance during World War II.

This is the Black Diamond, a 1928 Phantom I made to order for a diamond merchant.

The Rolls-Royce
trademark and logo

The Queen of England had this representation of Saint
George and a dragon placed as the hood ornament on her
Phantom VI.

GLOSSARY

cc – Cubic centimeters, used to measure engine size.

chassis (CHAS-ee) – The frame and mechanical parts of a car, excluding the body.

coach builder – A company that designs and builds only the bodies of cars.

coupe (KOOP) – A car with two doors.

Crewe (KREW) – The town in England where Rolls-Royces are made.

Hinduminum (hin-DEN-ee-em) – An aluminum alloy used by Rolls-Royce to make engines.

hp – Horsepower.

Legalimit – An early model Rolls-Royce that could go only 20 mph.

mm – Millimeter.

mph – Miles per hour.

right-hand drive – The British practice of placing the steering wheel on the right side of the car because traffic travels on the left side of the road in England.

The original Silver Ghost,
now on display at the Rolls-
Royce factory in Crewe

INDEX